toronto parks

This book has been published with the assistance of the following sponsors:

Provincial Papers, a subsidiary of Rolland inc
Matthews Ingham and Lake Fine Lithographers (A Quebecor Company)
Victor Beitner Systems Ltd
Zeta Media Inc
Dr. Agata Cybula Dental Clinic

We would like to heartily thank the following people for their contribution in bringing this book to life:

Annie-Lou Chester for her thoughtful critique and editing.
Staff of Metro Parks and Culture Department for providing map references
and comprehensive information on Metro Parks.
Zbyszek Kubica for sharing his technical knowledge of the production process.

toronto parks

Photographs • Andrzej Maciejewski

Illustrations • Teresa Mrozicka

Text • Sue Lebrecht

Introduction • Wayne Grady

KLOTZEK PRESS

First published in 1997 by
Klotzek Press
5 Doran Avenue
Toronto, Ontario, Canada M6S 2P7
phone/fax: (416) 766-0477

Canadian Cataloguing in Publication Data

Maciejewski, Andrzej, 1959-
        Toronto parks

Hardcover ISBN 0-9680657-2-4
Paperback ISBN 0-9680657-3-2

        1. Parks——Ontario——Toronto Metropolitan Area——
Pictorial works. 2. Toronto Metropolitan Area (Ont.)——
Pictorial works. I. Mrozicka, Teresa, 1962-
II. Lebrecht, Sue, 1962- III. Title.

FC3097.65.M33 1997 971.3'54104'0222 C97-900421-7
F1059.5.T687M33 1997

Printed by Matthews Ingham & Lake Inc (A Quebecor Company), Don Mills, Ontario
Paper by Provincial Papers, a subsidiary of Rolland inc, Thunder Bay, Ontario. (Jenson Gloss 100lb text)
Scans, film and separations by Victor Beitner Systems Ltd, Concord, Ontario
Book and cover design by Teresa Mrozicka

Trade distribution by
Firefly Books
3680 Victoria Park Avenue
Willowdale, Ontario, Canada M2H 3K1
phone: (416) 499-8412 fax: (416) 499-8313

Front cover photograph: Etienne Brulé Park, June 1995
Back cover map: High Park (fragment)

sitting quietly
doing nothing
spring comes
and the grass
grows by itself

The Zenrin

Moore Park Ravine, October 1994

CONTENTS

Toronto Parks explores 27 of the more than 1000 named parks within Metropolitan Toronto. The selection is diverse. It includes old parks that evolved with the city, land donations from private estates, and new man-made parks on the waterfront. It presents spacious grounds and small parcels; natural settings and fawned gardens. Some grace the business core, some are surrounded by residential neighbourhoods, a number lie in ravine valleys. As most touch water—along the lake shore and on the Don and Humber rivers— we've sectioned the book accordingly. Each park, however, is distinct and differently developed, radiating a character of its own.

Steeles Ave. E.

Finch Ave. E.

401

DVP

Eglinton Ave. E.

Kingston Rd.

Danforth Ave.

Scale: Kilometres

0 1 2 3 4 5

N

Metropolitan
Toronto Parks

1 Allan Gardens
2 Beaches Park
3 Coronation Park
4 Earl Bales Park
5 Edwards Gardens
6 Etienne Brulé Park
7 Grange Park
8 Guildwood Park
9 High Park
10 Home Smith Park
11 Humber Bay Park

12 James Gardens
13 Lambton Woods
14 Queen's Park
15 Rosedale Valley Ravine
16 Rosetta McClain Gardens
17 Rouge Park
18 Rouge Beach Park
19 Scarborough Bluffs
20 Serena Gundy Park
21 St. James Park
22 Sunnybrook Park
23 Taylor Creek Park
24 Toronto Island Park
25 Trinity Bellwoods Park
26 The Village of
    Yorkville Park
27 Wilket Creek Park

Budapest Park, September 1994

INTRODUCTION

I am sitting on my living room floor, surrounded by parks. I have taken an armload of brochures, very kindly sent to me by the department of Parks and Culture for Metro Toronto, and spread them out on the floor, imagining myself to be the corner of Bloor and Yonge. Just to the north of me are Wilket Creek Park and Edwards Gardens, with its fabulous nature and gardening library. To my right is Taylor Creek Park and the exotic greenhouses of Allan Gardens, and farther to my right are the magnificent Scarborough Bluffs. Looking left along Bloor, I can see the Humber River's Etienne Brulé Park and James Gardens. And behind me, Toronto Islands—one big park—and the Beaches.

I could go on and on. There are a lot of brochures. There are a lot of parks in Toronto. Within Metro alone there are more than 1,000 named municipal parks and 55 Metro parks—the names themselves are a living history of Toronto: Ernest Thompson Seton Park, Rosetta McClain Gardens, Betty Sutherland Trail, Charles Sauriol Conservation Reserve. If you include public gardens, golf courses, and cemeteries, Metro Toronto's open spaces add up to more than 10,000 hectares—17 percent of the total urban area, a much higher percentage than the North American average, which is around 5 percent. Although most of the municipal parks are smaller than a city block, they are still vital patches of green and well used. The Metro parks are bigger; the 10 largest ones are 100 hectares each. And they are getting bigger; the newly formed Rouge Park, which stretches from Lake Ontario to north of Steeles and includes the Metro Zoo and farmlands bypassed by development is more than 2,500 hectares in size and is the largest urban park in North America. Toronto is a city of parks. We have grown away from speaking of the Greater Toronto Area, and now think of ourselves as part of the Greater Toronto Bioregion.

For Torontonians know that a city is more than a mechanical construct of concrete and glass and steel, more even than a complex web of human interrelationships. A city is a habitat. It has an ecological as well as a technological being: it does not displace nature so much as nestle down beside it. Toronto, built over an intimate network of river valleys, ravines and lakefront, contains an abundance of wildlife that often exceeds that of the more rural areas that surround it. The raccoon population is denser in Toronto than it is in the forest; there are more skunks per hectare in Toronto than there are in Algonquin Park. Toronto has its own wild deer herd, and at least one pack of coyotes that keep the deer in check. There are at least 1,000 red foxes living south of Steeles. And don't even begin to count the pigeons, ring-billed gulls, Canada geese, mallards, buffleheads, hooded mergansers and wigeons that call Toronto home. Human beings have not supplanted nature in Toronto, they have merely joined it.

This notion of human beings joining nature is reflected in the design of the park system itself, for although Toronto's parks are in place for the protection of their natural habitat, they are also there to be used. While hiking up the Don Valley one August afternoon, I spoke to a man and his son who had cycled from their home in the Jane-Finch corridor, down the Humber Valley, along the Harbourfront, and were on their way back home via the west fork of the Don—they would have cycled for eight hours without leaving parkland. According to park authorities, the Metro Green Space System comprises more than 100 kilometres of major trails for cycling and walking and many times that when it comes to informal trails along rivers and through forests.

There are also parks for soccer or softball playing, parks for equestrians, and parks for the simple pleasure of nature observation. Rock hounds can read 90,000 years of geological history in the Scarborough Bluffs; birders know where the hawking is best; historians have earmarked stone foundations and millworks; botanists can spend whole days in fragments of the Carolinian forest; fishing for pike in the Don and salmon in the Humber is a historical pastime that has once again become possible, thanks to the diligence of conservation and park authorities. As Tommy Thompson, Toronto's first Parks

Commissioner and the man who coined the motto—"Please walk on the grass!"—expressed it in 1956, "Metropolitan parks should offer opportunities for an outdoor experience—a basic need of people—in a manner which they can enjoy." Thompson's goal has been amply realized in the forty years since he first expressed it.

This book is a wonderful distillation of Toronto's connection to its natural heritage. Andrzej Maciejewski's forty-nine sepia-toned photographs, taken over a period of several years, perfectly convey the unique combination of gentle peace and vital activity that is the essence of the urban park. Wordsworth defined poetry as "emotion recollected in tranquility," and these photographs are the visual equivalent of nature poetry. We often tend to think of a photograph as a static thing, just as we sometimes think of nature as still life: Andrzej's photographic images, like nature itself, magically enshrine movement and vitality. A faint blurr in the foreground where a cyclist has passed and left only a fleeting image on the plate; the subtle play of light from a path-lamp on a nodding blade of grass, stirred by the evening breeze we can almost see in the frame.

This book is more than a guide to Toronto's parks—though with its informative text and hand-drawn maps it is certainly that. It is a key by which we enter a world of light and movement, of life and moment, that we realize with a start has never been more than a few steps away, all the time.

—Wayne Grady

High Park

High Park is the city's largest park. What began with a 67 hectare donation in 1873 has became a 162 hectare oasis with subsequent land purchases by the city. The original core was a gift from John George Howard with conditions—among many—that no trees be removed and no "drinking booths or intoxicating liquor" be allowed on grounds.

A British-born architect and surveyor, Howard arrived in York with his wife Jemima in 1832. He worked as a drawing master at Upper Canada College, started a private architectural practice and became the first city surveyor and city engineer. The place he chose to call home was hilly land east of the Humber River overlooking Humber Bay. High Park, he called it. Here he built his house—one of the first in York with indoor plumbing—and named it after lieutenant governor Sir John Colborne, founder of Upper Canada College.

In the decades that followed, Howard hired a farmer to cultivate fodder crops on the estate while he designed the Lunatic Asylum at 999 Queen Street and the landscape of St. James Cemetery. After his death, Howard's house stood abandoned until the 1920s when it was restored. Today the Regency style house is a museum with period costumed staff offering tours of Victorian times.

Down the hill, Grenadier Pond is the city's only natural winter ice skating rink with ovals, streaks and rectangles shoveled snow-free by volunteers. Pleasure skaters, speed skaters and pick-up hockey enthusiasts all come to play. Stretching almost the length of the park, the pond supports more than a dozen species of fish including pike and bass. Fishing is allowed; keeping the catch is discouraged.

The pond was named after British Grenadier soldiers, posted at Fort York during the War of 1812, who held drills on the frozen surface and in the surrounding woods. At the time, only a sandbar separated the pond from Lake Ontario. Its marshy banks today are home to nesting waterfowl.

A neighbouring slope is decked with the Hillside Gardens, an elaborate display among rocks, hedges, streams and collection pools. At the hilltop, Grenadier Restaurant, the park's only eatery, is a popular neighbourhood meeting place. In the central ravine of the park are animal paddocks established in 1890.

Dream in High Park

1. Allotment Gardens
2. Animal Paddocks
3. Chess House
4. Colborne Lodge
5. The Dream Site
6. Forest School
7. Grenadier Restaurant
8. Greenhouses (not public)
9. Hillside Gardens
10. Howard Tomb
11. Martin Goodman Trail
12. Sports Complex

LEGEND

- J Telephone
- Wading pool
- S Snack bar
- Walking path
- Fire pit
- Trackless train station
- Washroom fully accessible

Scale: Metres
0   100   200   300

Bloor Street West

Soccer
Football
Outdoor Pool
Tennis
Tennis
Skating
Baseball
Tennis
Lawn Bowling

Colborne Lodge Dr.
Centre Rd.
Parkside
High Park Blvd.

Grenadier Pond

N

The Queensway
Gardiner Expressway
Lakeshore Blvd. W.

Today they hold buffaloes, llamas, highland cattle and Barbary and Moflon sheep.

What isn't obvious is the park's ecosystems. It has three distinct, overlapping forest regions. To the east is Boreal forest with northern white pine and white birch. On high, dry, sandy soil to the west, Carolinian forest—rare in Ontario—includes sassafras, white oak, black cherry, witch hazel, black walnut and wild lupine. In the middle is Prairie Savannah with widely spaced black oak trees and an understory of prairie grasses and wildflowers.

Three ravine systems carve the park's terrain. Sandy paths and woodchip trails traverse the steep and undulating interior. More than 200 bird species live in or pass through its habitat. A hawk watch takes place September through November, with birders on a knoll keeping count by the thousands.

Naturalists lead free Sunday walks, spring through fall on different themes from flower folklore to wild mushrooms and butterflies. Drummers gather informally and beat for hours on congas, bongos and other hand-drums in a field north of the restaurant. People attracted to the rhythm, watch and dance. Close to Bloor Street, the Chess Club building is host to quiet games year-round.

Approximately 600 dogs frequent the park daily with their masters. They are allowed to run free in two off-leash areas: between the Dream Site and the Allotment Gardens, and on Spring Road between Centre Road and the duck ponds.

At dusk in summer, an audience of 2,000-plus gather to watch Shakespearean theatre, presented by the Canadian Stage Company. New terraced seating faces the stage which is set in a backdrop of tall trees. Dream in High Park is a pay-what-you-can affair with donations accepted in big wooden boxes at the entrance gate. Lights come on, the play begins and before its over, stars are seen in the sky.

Just west of Colborne Lodge, iron fencing that once surrounded St. Paul's Cathedral in London, encloses a plot marked with a granite monument. Here, J.G. Howard and his wife rest in peace.

High Park, May 1996

High Park , August 1996

High Park, May 1992

High Park, March 1995

High Park, August 1996

Serena Gundy Park, June 1996

ALONG THE DON RIVER

Edwards Gardens

An intimate ravine, thousands of bulbs bloom on its slopes. Rhododendrons and azaleas colour its creek banks. Lilacs perfume paths.

Bring a grandparent and link arms. Wander softly; move slowly. From the parking lot, descend the paved path through refined gardens or choose the earthen trail through woods. Either way, when you reach the bottom, please, walk on the grass.

Pick a bench, any bench. Try the sunny hillside overlooking the arched bridge where a wedding reception is being photographed. Opt for the shade of a majestic oak amid a rock garden. Or sit beside Wilket Creek next to the waterwheel. Now inhale and relax.

When you're ready to stroll some more, explore the high ground on the ravine's west bank. Cross a bridge and ascend a shaded trail. The grassy upland features circular beds of roses and other brilliant flowers.

The Civic Centre, next to the parking lot, features an outstanding horticultural library, a gift store, garden shop and a master gardener information line. It's also home to the Garden Club of Toronto and a hub of activity. Sign up for a course on floral arranging, rock gardening or landscape design; listen to a lecture on horticultural therapy or garden artistry; visit annual shows presented by the Mycological, Ikebana and Southern Ontario Orchid societies. In summer, the Centre offers free tours of the park daily.

Alexander Milne originally settled this land in 1817. It stayed in his family for over a century. Then in 1944, after a series of owners, it became a country home to a wealthy paint manufacturer, Rupert E. Edwards. He spent his first three summers constructing a 150-metre-long rock garden, and then built curved paths, extensive flower beds, rustic bridges, a fountain and wishing well. After 12 years, as surrounding farmland gave way to residential homes, Edwards sold his property to the city for a mere $153,000. Metro Toronto Parks opened it to the public in June 1956 and ever since, Edwards Gardens has offered immersion into peace.

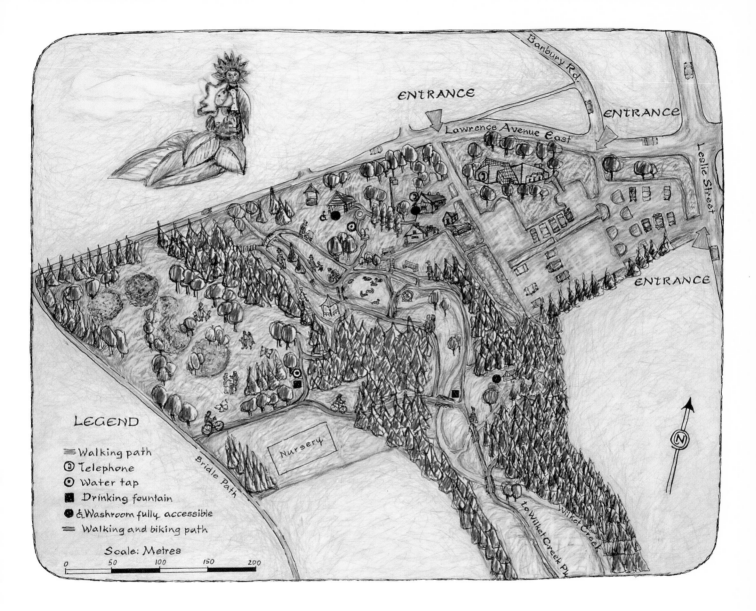

ENTRANCE

Banbury Rd.

Lawrence Avenue East

ENTRANCE

Leslie Street

ENTRANCE

Nursery

Bridle Path

to Wilket Creek Pk.

Wilket Creek

LEGEND

Walking path
③ Telephone
⊙ Water tap
▪ Drinking fountain
● &Washroom fully accessible
Walking and biking path

Scale: Metres

0   50   100   150   200

N

Edwards Gardens, May 1996

Edwards Gardens, October 1994

Sunnybrook Park • Wilket Creek Park
Serena Gundy Park

Wilket Creek Park begins where Edwards Gardens ends, where a bridge transfers path followers from prim grounds to natural surrounds. The deep narrow valley shimmers between steep walls of leaves in summer and reveals its rolling upper contours behind tree trunks in winter. The creek zig zags among shrubs and cattails while the paved trail, for both cyclists and walkers, cuts a straight line over numerous bridges.

The valley was first settled by Alexander Milne in 1812 and was known as Milne Creek until the 1950s. A wooden staircase on the west bank ascends the tree and wildflower strewn slope. At the top, among oak, maple and beech, an earthen trail leads to Sunnybrook Park.

Originally the country estate of Joseph Kilgour in the late 1800s, Sunnybrook Park was site to the first Provincial Plowing Match in 1913, and—thanks to the Toronto Field Naturalists—to the first urban wilderness trail in 1930. Its huge plateau was a favourite campground for Boy Scouts and a transit camp for troops preparing for Europe during the Second World War.

Today, the flat, open upland is dominated by a massive sports field capable of hosting more than half a dozen separate games of cricket, soccer, rugby and field hockey. Hidden in the bordering trees, a fitness trail loops the highland.

Down the access road is the English style horseback riding stable, Sunnybrook. Spectators are welcome to watch riding lessons at the outdoor paddock and periodic equestrian competitions. Further down, the road meets the West Don River, meadows with picnic tables and barbecue sites, and a 100-year-old log cabin that serves as a nature study centre. Hey, look, see the fox in the trees?

Serena Gundy Park is named after the first wife of the late James Gundy, president of the securities dealer Wood Gundy Limited and former owner of the land. Situated on the south side of the West Don, it is accessible by a wooden foot bridge as well as a large suspension bridge. It's a narrow, quiet and intimate park with statuesque trees in open fields and high banks dropping to the river.

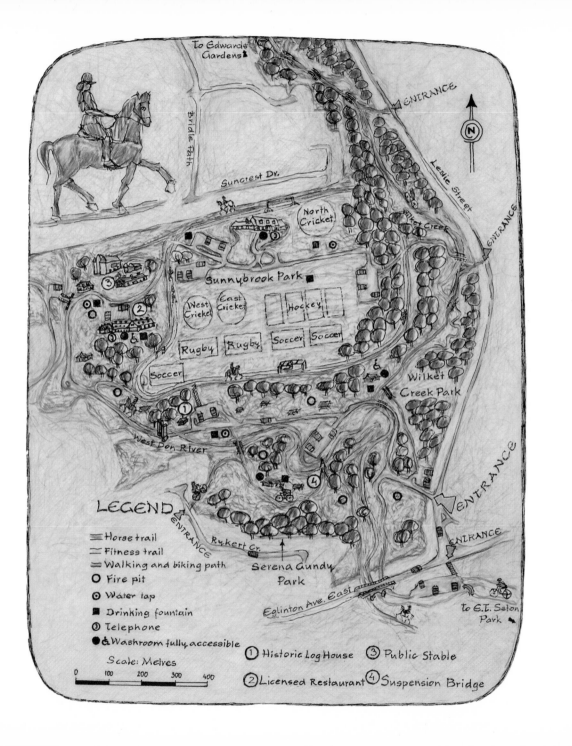

To Edwards Gardens

ENTRANCE

Bridle Path

Suncrest Dr.

Leslie Street

Wilket Creek

North Cricket

Sunnybrook Park

West Cricket

East Cricket

Hockey

Rugby

Rugby

Soccer

Soccer

Soccer

Wilket Creek Park

West Don River

ENTRANCE

ENTRANCE

ENTRANCE

Rykert Cr.

Serena Gundy Park

ENTRANCE

Eglinton Ave. East

To E.T. Seton Park

LEGEND

Horse trail
Fitness trail
Walking and biking path
Fire pit
Water tap
Drinking fountain
Telephone
Washroom fully accessible

Scale: Metres

0   100   200   300   400

① Historic Log House   ③ Public Stable
② Licensed Restaurant   ④ Suspension Bridge

Serena Gundy Park, June 1996

Sunnybrook Park, May 1996

Sunnybrook Park, May 1996

Wilket Creek Park, May 1992

Taylor Creek Park

Snapshots catch your eye while cycling the paved trail beside the creek. Great blazes of bulrushes glowing golden in the sunshine, an old tree, gnarled and twisted in a bed of grass. A wispy willow in an open field, gracious lawn beside a tangle of shrubs against a backdrop of trunks. The base of a staircase rising through woods.

As you pedal through the valley bottom, framed in steep, tree-shaded slopes, the creek curves slightly and forever out-of-view. High branches sway. But the sensation of wind is not felt, only seen and heard.

You stop on a bridge and lean against the rail. Trees arch over the flowing water. Layers of carefully laid rock bound in wire mesh line the banks of the creek. Red and white trilliums grow wild.

From the base of Don Mills Road to Victoria Park Avenue, Taylor Creek Park offers a 5-km-long ride on a level path shared by cyclists, joggers, in-line skaters and walkers. In winter, it is used by cross-country skiers. In spring, more than 200 species of birds fly through the park's corridor.

Beginning at the confluence of three rivers known as the Forks of the Don, the path is an extension to trails along the Don River, while the creek is a major tributary. Cross the many footbridges to wander either side. Alternatively, concrete fords invite you to walk through the water, ankle deep.

The park is named after the Taylor brothers, who in 1834 established saw and paper mills in the area which became extremely productive by the 1900s. The tributary, however, is called Massey Creek. In 1897, Walter Massey purchased about 100 hectacres of surrounding land and operated a farm that produced milk to help combat typhoid fever among city children.

Picnic tables, barbecue pits, water fountains and washroom facilities are scattered throughout the park. Street signs are posted at path intersections. A fitness trail instructs interested participants to do log jumps, elevated push ups, torso twists and more. Benches under trees invite sitting. But from the seat of your bike, the trail lures you onward.

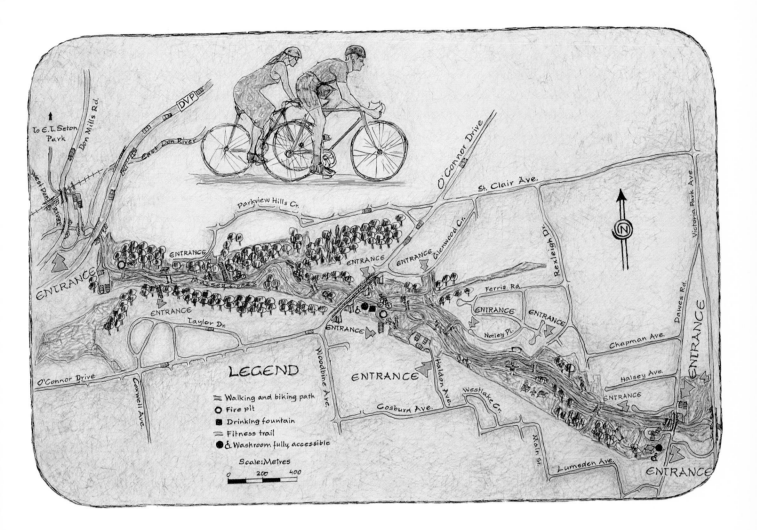

LEGEND

≋ Walking and biking path
○ Fire pit
▣ Drinking fountain
≡ Fitness trail
● ♿ Washroom fully accessible

Scale: Metres

0   200   400

Taylor Creek Park, October 1994

Taylor Creek Park, November 1996

Earl Bales Park

In winter, music wafts from loud speakers over the ski hill. A novelty in the city, the North York Ski Centre has three treeless trails on the valley slope. The vertical drop, 39 metres, is tiny by any ski resort standard, but day and night, it's well-used for racing, freestyle, telemark skiing, snowboarding and even classes for the disabled.

The chalet, positioned at the top of the chairlift, is a short walk from the parking lot. Lifts tickets, snacks and refreshments may be bought here. At the hilltop, a sign on a tree says "No Tobogganing". Below in the quiet basin, cross-country skiers glide and the West Don River river flows.

In summer, live music, dance and theatre attract crowds to the outdoor Barry Zuckerman Amphitheatre. Perched beside the ski chalet, the 1500 seats overflow when the Toronto Symphony, Royal Winnipeg Ballet, The Flying Bulgar Klezmer Band, and other popular groups perform.

In eerie contrast, the Holocaust memorial near the Bathurst Street entrance begs attention. Dark and withered, it looks disturbingly like a burnt tree, stripped of its branches. Beside it stands the bust of Raoul Wallenberg, the Swedish diplomat who risked his life and saved tens of thousands of Jews from death. The monuments reflect the strong Jewish community within North York.

Tucked out of view in the park's northwest corner is the homestead of John Bales, built in 1824. The original owner and settler of the property, he was the great grandfather of Robert Earl Bales who was elected reeve of the Township of North York in 1934 and later became chairman of the North York's planning board.

For a quiet nature stroll, follow the paved trail near the amphitheatre down to the river. Continue downstream past a cedar grove, across an open field to the sugar maple forest in the southwest. Or walk upstream, out of the park, under the high bridge of Sheppard Avenue, to West Don Parklands. Here, a path meanders through meadow, then woods where side trails beckon and hidden birds watch.

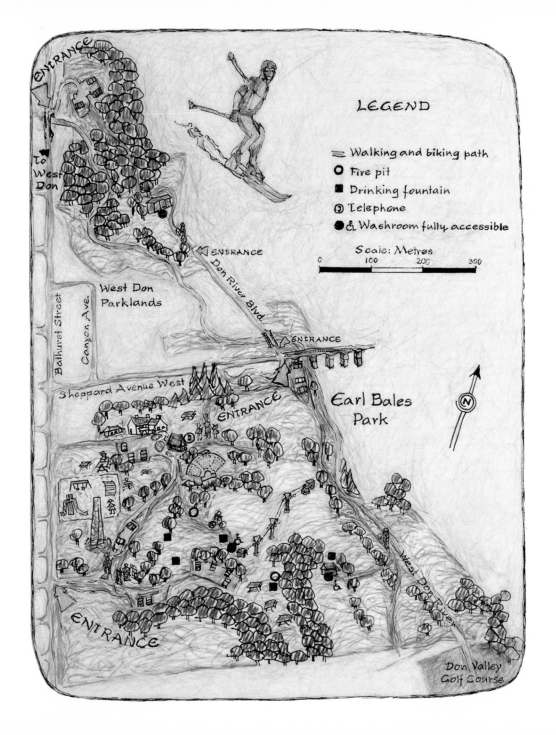

LEGEND

━━ Walking and biking path
○ Fire pit
■ Drinking fountain
☎ Telephone
● ♿ Washroom fully accessible

Scale: Metres
0   100   200   300

Entrance
To West Don
West Don Parklands
Bathurst Street
Canyon Ave.
Don River Blvd.
Entrance
Entrance
Sheppard Avenue West
Entrance
Entrance
Earl Bales Park
Entrance
West Don River
Don Valley Golf Course
N

Earl Bales Park, January 1995

Earl Bales Park, January 1995

Rowntree Mills Park, October 1994

ALONG THE HUMBER RIVER

Flagstone walkways lead the way among beautiful formal gardens. Wooden bridges cross over spring-fed pools. Elegant pines, fern groves and a gazebo grace the grounds. On the west bank of the Humber River, James Gardens, site of numerous wedding receptions, requires dodging to avoid being caught in a photographer's flash.

History isn't immediately apparent. One has to look deep into a pool to see former bathing steps; high on the hillside to see the old estate home; close in the rose bushes to read the memorial to Frederick T. James and his wife.

A wholesale fish merchant who operated a market where the parking lot is today, James began to transform this property when he purchased it from his wife's parents in 1908. Using Humber River slate and weeping tiles to create terraces and collection pools, he built a garden where visitors were then—as now—welcome.

From the formal gardens, a paved path leads to the edge of the Humber River. Here one can continue north or south. Walking south, with the river's flow, you'll seamlessly enter another park, Lambton Woods. The path rises up an embankment to a cliff edge with a grand river view.

But there's another, more enchanting entrance into Lambton, just before the river's edge. Where trimmed lawn meets pristine forest, an earthen trail edged with logs leads through a tunnel of trees. Sounds diminish. Hardwoods surround. Wildflowers skirt tiny creeks that trickle through lush growth. An array of birds squabble about a hanging feeder and brave chickadees take prize sunflower seeds from the hands of patient observers.

Continuing south, one enters a cathedral of towering trees. All is quiet, the air is cool. Ahead, a railway trestle stretches high over the Humber River while a wooden footbridge underneath proceeds to the east bank. Here, old foundations of a former bridge can be seen.

In the mid-1800s, the Village of Lambton Mills was a thriving community of about 500 people at the river crossing below Dundas Street. The Village was named after the local saw mill which was named after the first Earl of Durham, John George Lambton, in honour of his visit.

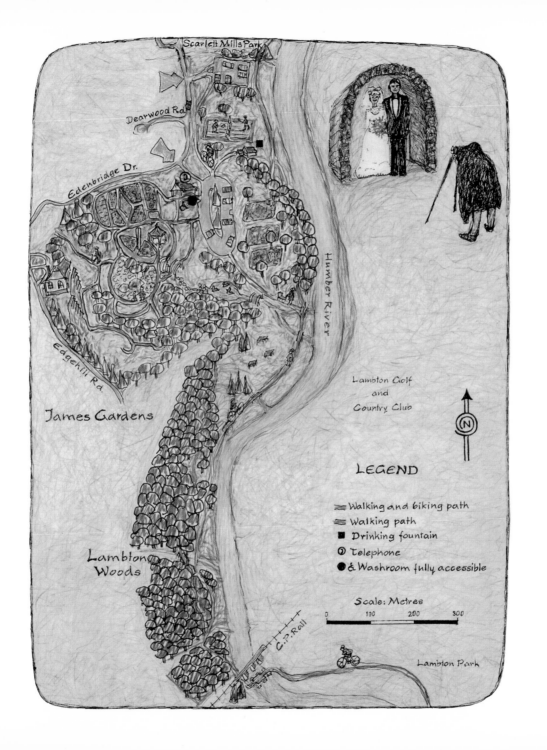

Lambton Woods, October 1996

James Gardens, November 1996

Etienne Brulé was 20 years old in 1615 when he stood at the mouth of the Humber River and became the first European to see Lake Ontario. He had travelled with a band of Huron Indians from Lake Simcoe down the Humber River Valley on an 45-km-long portage route known as the Carrying-Place Trail. Ancient and foot-worn by native people, the route became an important passageway to the north and contributed to the positioning of Toronto.

Jesuit missionaries shunned Brulé for adopting Indian ways, and Huron Indians killed him in 1633. From Dundas Street south to Old Mill Road on the east bank of the Humber River, the park is named in his honour.

A paved path is set to the sound of falling water. As you walk with the river's flow, one dam after another creates a rush that resonates across fields of green. The valley narrows, then widens. You pass a grove of apple trees. A serenade follows.

Deceivingly tame most days, the Humber runs wild with spring runoff and after each rainfall. When Hurricane Hazel ripped through the area in 1954, the river rose six metres, sweeping away 14 homes on Raymore Drive and killing 32 residents in one hour. Fortified river banks, angled rock walls and dams were built in an effort to control its might. But even in recent winters, adjacent fields have been covered with jagged slabs of upheaved ice that left scars high on trees.

Nearly hidden, a wooden staircase leads up the steep valley to Baby Point. This is the ancient site of a large Iroquois village that feasted on the salmon that ran thick here until the mid-1800s. Today, in autumn, fishermen line the base of the dam closest to the old mill bridge, casting for the arms-length sized salmon that struggle upstream to spawn.

On the opposite shore, Home Smith Park, tightly framed by valley walls, has a one-way road running through it. Picnic tables and barbecue sites welcome visitors to simply sit and eat beside the river's bank.

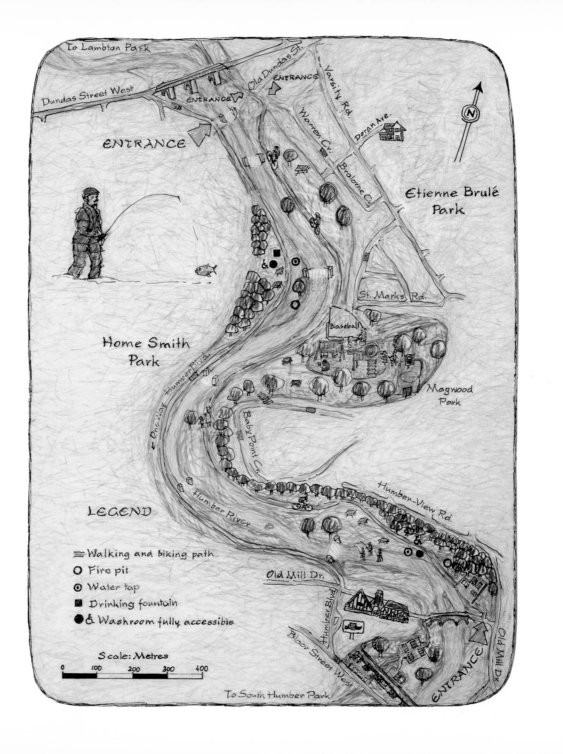

Etienne Brulé Park, June 1995

Étienne Brulé Park , May 1992

Home Smith Park, May 1992

Etienne Brulé Park, September 1995

Allan Gardens, January 1995

DOWNTOWN

Downtown

Small yet intensely used, Toronto downtown parks are niches for play and tranquility. Each has a distinct character, linked to its site, inception, evolution and neighbourhood.

Queen's Park, an oval crowning the top of University Avenue, is home to the Ontario Parliament Buildings. Here, thousands have gathered both in protest and celebration. Behind the legislature is green space with mature trees where in summer, music, theatre and multi-cultural festivals take place. Students from the surrounding University of Toronto keep the grounds alive from dawn to dusk.

St. James Park is site of the city's first home for Christian worship. What began with a small church in 1807, is now the elegant St. James' Cathedral. Its clock bells chime on the quarter hour, and organ concerts are offered free on Tuesday afternoons. An arched entrance welcomes visitors to the adjacent park which consists of a garden, a gazebo and modern sculpture among grass-covered mounds. The garden, an original 19th-century English style, has low shrubs, blooming perennials, a water fountain and statue of Cupid. A dainty iron gate begs entrance;

God's Garden, it's called. A poem on a sign concludes "one is nearer to God in a garden than anywhere else on earth".

Allan Gardens features a conservatory, open free year-round. Flagstone pathways lead from one greenhouse to another, from the tropics to the desert, through six different settings. Palm trees thrive in a high-domed enclosure, orchids and begonias bloom, jasmine and narcissus perfume the humid air. All thanks to politician George Allan who gave the Toronto Horticultural Society this parcel of land in 1858. First, a rustic pavilion was built, then an elaborate iron, wood and glass structure, which sadly was destroyed by fire. Today's domed Palm House, built in 1909, is an extraordinary reminder of old splendor.

Trinity-Bellwoods Park welcomes visitors off Queen Street through the relic of a stone gate, the last remains of Trinity College, demolished in 1956. Established in the name of religion, Trinity was the realized goal of Bishop Strachan, head of King's College. Outraged at the new "Godless" creation of the University of Toronto in 1849, he petitioned for a new Anglican university. On site today, Portuguese seniors play cards on warm days while kids cool off

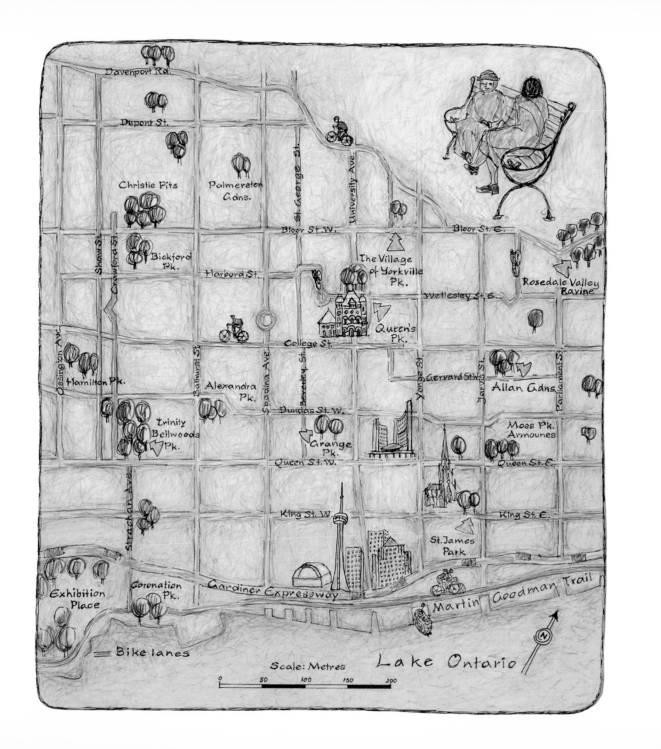

in the wading pool. In the park's centre, a deep depression makes for great tobogganing in winter. A creek used to run through it, but now flows hidden underground.

Grange Park is named after the Georgian-styled house with its columned porch, shuttered windows and elegant symmetry. The Grange (an English term meaning "gentleman's residence"), was built in dense forest of a 100-acre estate by D'Arcy Boulton in 1817. Backing the Art Gallery of Ontario and the Ontario College of Art, the building is open with tours by period costumed interpreters. What remains of the estate, bordered in gracious iron fencing, is a small rectangular park with old chestnut trees. Local Chinese women practice Tai Chi on the lawn, kids play in a sandbox and art students sketch.

The Village of Yorkville Park manages to present a crabapple orchard, prairie wildflowers, Ontario marsh, and ten other slices of distinct landscape, all in less than half a hectare. The result of a 1991 international design competition won by Oleson Worland Architects, this unusual tableau complements the former hippie hangout of Yorkville, now an upscale district of fancy restaurants, art galleries and designer fashion boutiques. With its simulated waterfall, a 650-tonne of Muskoka rock—transported and reassembled— twinkling lights and induced mist, the park is intriguing day or night.

Rosedale Valley Ravine blushed with blooms of wild roses and a creek ran through it. Deep, long and narrow, the ravine isolated the mansions of Rosedale from residential Toronto south of Bloor until an access road was built in the early 1900s. Home owner Edgar John Jarvis later constructed a bridge over the valley on Glen Road. Offering a stunning sight each autumn, pedestrians, not carriages, use it today. Far below, Rosedale Valley Road traces the ravine's groove. A paved path beside it offers a good long walk or bike ride under the cool canopy of leaves, all the way to the Don River and its valley trail.

The Village of Yorkville Park, October 1996

Queen's Park, June 1995

Grange Park, November 1996

Trinity Bellwoods Park, June 1995

Allan Gardens, January 1997

Rosedale Valley Ravine, May 1995

St. James Park, November 1996

Sunnyside Beach Park, September 1994

WATER FRONT

Humber Bay Park

68

Coronation Park

72

Toronto Island Park

76

Beaches Park

82

Rouge Park
Rouge Beach Park

82

Scarborough Bluffs
Guildwood Park
Rosetta McClain
Gardens

90

Humber Bay Park

Embracing the mouth of Mimico Creek with two outstretched arms, Humber Bay Park is a place to play and muse.

Action takes place on the east arm. Hobbyists on tiered benches steer remote control boats on three ponds, kite flyers in adjacent fields maneuver wings on strings in an offshore wind, and fishermen on a long pier cast lines for salmon and trout.

Crushed limestone trails lead hikers among tall grass and slender trees to far points of the landspit. Stepping stones across an inland channel give access to a circular field framed by a crescent of large rocks. A plaque says the rocks in this park come from the Niagara Escarpment and consist almost entirely of fossilized shells and skeletons of marine invertebrate which lived 410 million years ago.

Stacked boulders serve as a shore break on far points while waves lick pebbly beaches in alcoves. Waterfowl rest and feed in recesses and the Toronto skyline looms in the distance.

The west side, by contrast, is a quiet place to watch sailboats and to have a quiet picnic among groves of trees. A road runs past several yacht clubs, two boat launch sites and the Metro Police Marine Unit.

It then curves to a tip graced by a red and white navigation light. A short walking trail loops a protected thumb of land and roams a cove. Onwards, an exposed stretch of grass leads to the lake's edge.

Built with lakefill and opened in 1984, Humber Bay Park protrudes in a bay that once sheltered American warships preparing to raid the Parliament Building during the War of 1812. It also borders a site known in the mid-1800s as Humber Bay Village which featured a strip of hotels including the Royal Oak and Wimbledon House. Then as now, flocks of migrating birds congregate at the creek's mouth. Named Mimico, it comes from the Mississauga Indian word Omineca, meaning home of the wild pigeons.

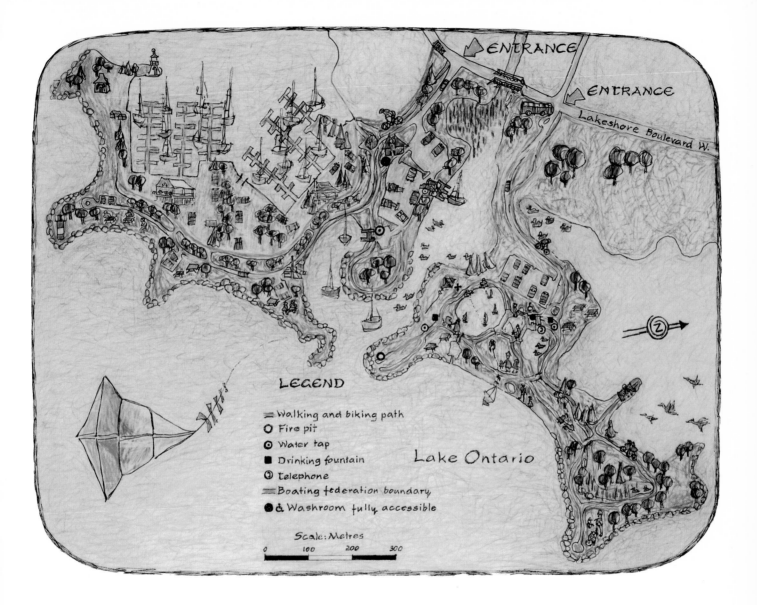

ENTRANCE

ENTRANCE

Lakeshore Boulevard W.

LEGEND

≡ Walking and biking path
○ Fire pit
◉ Water tap
■ Drinking fountain
Ⓣ Telephone
━━ Boating federation boundary,
●& Washroom fully accessible

Lake Ontario

Scale: Metres

0   100   200   300

Humber Bay Park, November 1996

Humber Bay Park, July 1996

Coronation Park

At first glance Coronation Park looks simply like green space with grand trees. But if you look more closely you'll notice that the trees form lines; paired lines mostly, some straight, others in sweeping curves. Each tree has a plaque at its base and many are encircled with grey stones. At the park's centre, in a looped paved path, majestic maples form a ring around an oak.

Coronation Park is in fact a memorial to Canadian soldiers who served in World War I. Its design is symbolic. The lines of trees, standing strong like uniformed troops, are a memorial to the 150 units of the Canadian Expeditionary Force. The royal oak at the centre pays tribute to King George VI. The surrounding ring of maples symbolizes countries of the British Empire.

Inspiration for the park came from "Men of Trees", an international organization founded by Richard St. Barbe Barker. It was Barker's dream that the planting of trees— the fostering of life—would temper political dissension. He hoped to soften world's hearts through the promotion of reforestation. The trees for Coronation Park were ceremoniously planted by Canadian war veterans in 1937. Sadly, the gesture laid roots only two years before the outbreak of the Second World War.

A Lancaster Bomber rests adjacent to the trees in a bare field. Similar to hundreds of planes flown by Canadian pilots during World War II, it was used for search-and-rescue missions until 1964.

By the shore stands a peace sculpture built on the 50th anniversary of the ending of World War II. In the likeness of ship, upright steel plates form V-shapes on either end of a circular formation of white blocks. In the very centre lies a medallion of the word "Peace" in 50 languages.

Waves wash against the seawall, an unseen sun casts a low glow on the lake's horizon, an elderly man scrapes overgrown grass away from a tree's plaque, and the Canadian Flag flaps in the wind.

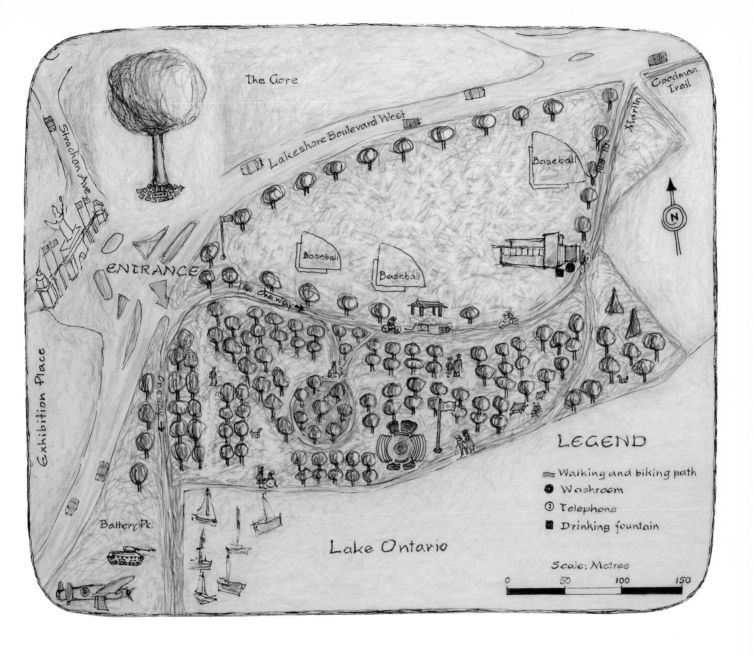

The Gore

Strachan Ave.

King

Lakeshore Boulevard West

Baseball

Martin

Goodman
Trail

N

ENTRANCE

Baseball

Baseball

Exhibition Place

one way

one way

Battery Pk.

LEGEND

Walking and biking path

Washroom

Telephone

Drinking fountain

Lake Ontario

Scale: Metres

0   50   100   150

Coronation Park, May 1995

Coronation Park, January 1995

Toronto Island Park

It began as peninsula, sandy with dunes and lagoons, sparsely vegetated. Crescent-shaped and pointing west, it was created with sediment from the Scarborough Bluffs. Waves eroded the bluffs, currents carried sand and gravel to the mouth of the Don River and accumulated over thousands of years.

To the Indians, the peninsula held healing powers. To John Graves Simcoe, the first lieutenant-governor of Upper Canada, its natural harbour directed the location for his capital city, York, established in 1793.

A lighthouse was erected at Gibraltar Point in 1809. With the elite of York seeking respite on sweltering summer days, a carriage route developed along its length. By the mid-19th century, the spit was home to a successful commercial fishing colony.

Nature continued to sculpt the land. The shoreline, ever-changing, had extended a km northwest and 400 m south of the lighthouse. In 1858, a gale lashed the peninsula's eastern arm, severing its connection to the mainland. Hence, "The Island" was born.

City dwellers visited in droves. A ferry powered by horses on treadmills shuttled people back and forth. Wealthy families built gracious Victorian homes. A summer community of tents and shacks sprang up. Trees were planted, lagoons were dredged. A church, schoolhouse, stores and waterworks were constructed.

Fisherman John Hanlan built a big hotel at the northwest end in 1878. Two years later, his son Ned built a magnificent second structure. The tip became known as Hanlan's Point and Ned became a world-champion rower. On the east end, William Ward, son of homesteader David Ward, built Ward's Hotel.

The late 1880s to 1920s were festive times. Large side wheelers and paddle steamers ferried crowds ashore. There were floating bathhouses, dance pavilions and a boardwalk. Hanlan's Point featured a 10,000-seat baseball stadium from which Babe Ruth hit his first professional home run in September 1914. Best of all, there was a grand amusement park. Step right up! See the 230-kg fat lady from South Africa in the "great and only museum of living curiosities". Watch J.W. Gorman's incredible diving horses. Ride the merry-go-round and "Figure Eight" rollercoaster.

The frolic ground to a halt, however, in the 1930s. An airport paved the ballpark,

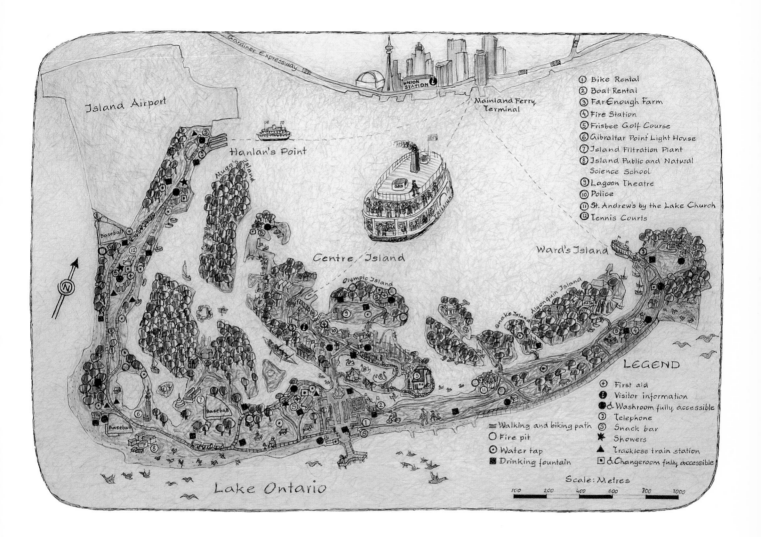

Island Airport

Gardiner Expressway

UNION STATION

Mainland Ferry Terminal

Hanlan's Point

Mugg's Island

Baseball

Centre Island

Olympic Island

Ward's Island

Snake Island

Algonquin Island

Baseball

Baseball

Lake Ontario

1 Bike Rental
2 Boat Rental
3 Far Enough Farm
4 Fire Station
5 Frisbee Golf Course
6 Gibraltar Point Light House
7 Island Filtration Plant
8 Island Public and Natural Science School
9 Lagoon Theatre
10 Police
11 St. Andrew's by the Lake Church
12 Tennis Courts

LEGEND

First aid
Visitor information
Washroom fully accessible
Telephone
Snack bar
Showers
Trackless train station
Changeroom fully accessible

Walking and biking path
Fire pit
Water tap
Drinking fountain

Scale: Metres
100   200   400   600   800   1000

the amusement park was demolished and the Great War came. With the ensuing housing shortage, nearly 2,000 people took up permanent residence on the Island.

In 1956, the city proper gave Toronto Island to Metropolitan Toronto for park development. Eviction notices were given and buildings were razed. Residents banded together in what would become an ongoing battle to save their homes and community.

Today, the Island is a recreational hot spot once again. Ferries carry 1.2 million passengers to its shores annually. Group picnics fill grassy expanses and people from a multitude of cultural backgrounds mingle.

Families head for Centreville with its bumper cars, swan paddleboats, and pony rides. A seven-km-long, car-free road from Ward's Island to Hanlan's Point presents the best in-line skating stretch in the city. On the southeast edge, a nearly two-km-long boardwalk offers a quiet stroll, even on busy weekends. A disc golf course, for throwing a Frisbee from one basket to the next, is free to use on Ward's Island. On Centre Island, a cedar hedge maze lures the curious. Built in 1967 as a Centennial Project, the maze challenges adults and kids alike.

Bike rentals include tandems and quadra cycles. Rental canoes offer exploration of interconnecting lagoons. Magnificent willows grace the grounds. Masses of migratory birds take refuge in its wetland; the Island is one of the city's best spots for birding. Beaches are everywhere, some strewn with driftwood, a few secluded.

History permeates. The Gibraltar Point lighthouse—Toronto's oldest stone structure and Canada's second oldest lighthouse— still stands, haunted by its first keeper. A community of about 750 people— including the Ward family and a high percentage of artists—live in quaint, wooden cottages, on carless streets on Ward's and Algonquin islands. High grass covers old foundations. Rows of trees are all that remain of some former avenues. The 1910 Trillium side-paddlewheeler has been restored to ferry service, thanks to the efforts historian Mike Filey.

But in the quiet of night, heading home on the ferry, Toronto's impressive skyline seems surreal—futuristic.

Toronto Island Park , August 1996

Toronto Island Park, August 1996

Toronto Island Park, May 1996

Beaches Park

A little more than a century ago, it was cottage country. Separated from the city by the Don River and providing cool relief on humid summer days, "The Beach" was a retreat. Toronto's elite built a resort community of breezy clapboard houses along the lakeshore. Women strolled along the boardwalk with sun parasols; men swam in elbow-to-knee cotton-knit bathing suits. There were amusement grounds, canoe clubs, hotels and an elitist attitude.

When the Toronto Street Railway created easier access in the 1890s, cottages were winterized into permanent homes and visitors flocked to the area. Today, it is one of Toronto's most popular tourist districts and residential neighbourhoods. Its three-km-long boardwalk, stretching along various named beaches, is a stroll through history unseen.

Kew Gardens, with its gazebo-staged concerts, old oaks and maples, was a farm owned by Joseph Williams. He made it a private park in 1879 and named it after the botanical gardens in London, England. He also named his son Kew, who in 1902, built the impressive stone house at the foot of Lee Avenue. The city expropriated the land in 1907.

The Beach had several amusement parks. One of the first stood where the R.C. Harris Filtration Plant is today. East of Kew Gardens, Scarboro Beach attracted thousands from 1907 to 1925 with its midway, tunnel of love and "chutes lagoon" slide. Here, American aviator Charles Willard presented Torontonians to their first air show. As he launched his Golden Flyer, the crowd swarmed the beach runway in glee, forcing him to splash down in the lake.

The 1920 wooden Leuty Lifeguard Station is still used today, and the Balmy Beach Club, a community institution since 1905, is a popular site for beach volleyball. A block north, Queen Street features an eclectic mix of shops, cafés and restaurants.

The park is crowded on weekends. Streams of people stroll the boardwalk. Cyclists and in-line skaters roll on a parallel paved path. Windsurfers streak across Ashbridges Bay. Donald D. Summerville Olympic Pools, with its 10-metre-high diving platform, provides an alternative to the now polluted lake. Long benches facing the water invite peaceful sitting.

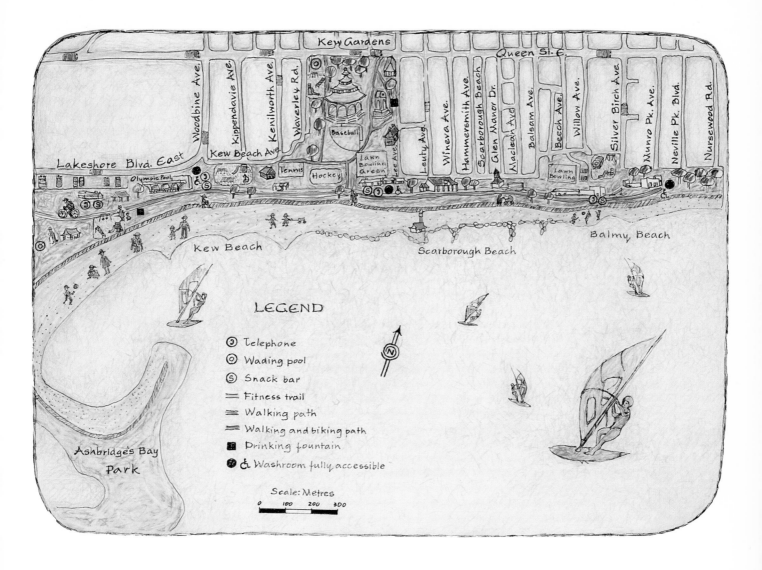

Beaches Park, October 1994

Beaches Park, July 1996

Rouge Park • Rouge Beach Park

A chorus of birds at dawn, an owl's hoot at dusk. A clifftop trail with a view and a welcoming flat rock beside the river's flow. A great blue heron steps gingerly among reeds and a white-tailed deer watches people stroll through forest. A wilderness experience at the city's east end, Rouge Park.

From the marshy shore of Lake Ontario north to the Oak Ridges Moraine roughly at Stouffville Side Road, Rouge Park is the largest urban park in North America. Encompassing the 35-km-long Rouge River and its tributaries, it is 29 times the size of High Park while its northern limits are still expanding.

Wetlands, woodlands, valleys, meadows and farmlands provide a home for 762 plant species—six of which are rare in Ontario—55 species of fish, 27 species of mammals, 123 species of birds and 19 reptiles and amphibians. In addition, its boundaries embrace the Metro Zoo, a private campground, a horseback riding stable, and the 125-year-old Pearse House that now serves as the park's visitors centre.

Fishermen cast lines in the marsh near the lakeshore while canoeists and kayakers paddle the river's lower end. People stroll along the beach and hike myriad unmarked and unmapped trails that lace the interior. Well-trodden paths touch the river's edge and run along the valley bottom through mature forests of white pine, white cedar, hemlock, sugar maple and beech. They lead through meadows past stone walls and apple trees dating back to pioneer days, and up along the river-carved bluff. Trails fork and branch in all directions, endlessly tempting the curious.

What was once a well used native canoe and portage route to the province's interior, and also a site where Mennonites from Pennsylvania settled after the America War of Independence in 1776, is now an ecosystem being nurtured. The endangered eastern bluebird and Cooper's hawk have returned. Habitat restoration efforts hope to bring back the Atlantic salmon, river otter and osprey. Carolinian forest species, common in the southern United States but rare in Canada, survive here, including witch hazel, black walnut and shy bulrush. Spring flowers flourish. Coyotes roam. The river runs. A sanctuary, Rouge Park.

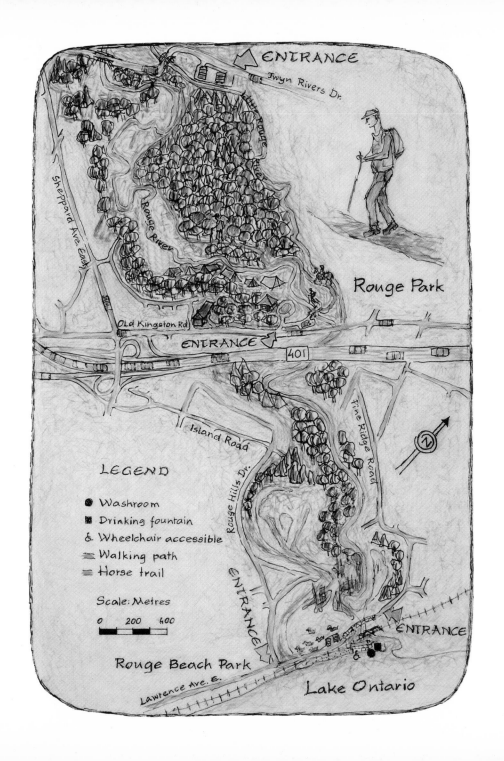

ENTRANCE

Jwyn Rivers Dr.

Sheppard Ave. East

Rouge River

Rouge Park

Old Kingston Rd

ENTRANCE

401

Island Road

Pine Ridge Road

Rouge Hills Dr.

N

LEGEND

● Washroom
■ Drinking fountain
& Wheelchair accessible
━ Walking path
━ Horse trail

Scale: Metres

0   200   400

ENTRANCE

ENTRANCE

Rouge Beach Park

Lake Ontario

Lawrence Ave. E.

Rouge Beach Park, November 1996

Rouge Park, November 1996

Scarborough Bluffs • Guildwood Park
Rosetta McClain Gardens

The Scarborough Bluffs are a gigantic cliff. Ten km in length, they peak at 90 metres near the mid-point at Cathedral Bluffs Park. Ravaged by wind and water, ever-eroding, the sandstone face features sheer drops, sloping ridges and tall, windsculpted spires.

Ancient layers of sand and clay record its history. During the Ice Age, the shifting of the Wisconsin Glacier left sedimentary deposits here. About 10,000 years ago the ice melted, creating Lake Iroquois, and the cliffs were a shoreline. As the water dropped to the present level of Lake Ontario, the cliff face was exposed. When the wife of Upper Canada's first Lieutenant Governor saw them in 1793, she named them after the white cliffs at Scarborough in Yorkshire, England. A succession of parks along their length welcomes you to explore.

Rosetta McClain Gardens, with its showcase of rose beds, was donated to the city in 1958 by Robert McClain in memory of his wife. The park is acclaimed for its accessibility with adjustable benches for the disabled and signs in braille.

The best place to see sandstone turrets is at Scarborough Bluffs Park. Walk on the edge through high grass and shrubbery for an impressive view of them. Irregular formations, they are a striking contrast to Bluffer's Park, far below. Jutting into Lake Ontario, this grassy manmade park, offers paved walkways around coves where yachts are moored, and access to a trail along the cliff base.

Guildwood Park is an eccentric outdoor museum of architecture and sculpture. Former estate owners Spencer and Rosa Clark rescued more than 70 building artifacts from Toronto's demolition days in the 1960s and '70s. Greek columns from the old Bank of Toronto building stand among pines, the arched entrance to the former Granite Club is draped in maples. A forested trail beckons to one side and a wooden staircase leads down to the lake.

Where the bluffs begin to diminish, the headland of East Point Park extends its wetland to migrating birds and butterflies. In a streak on the horizon, pale blue sky meets dark blue lake before the setting sun casts both ablaze.

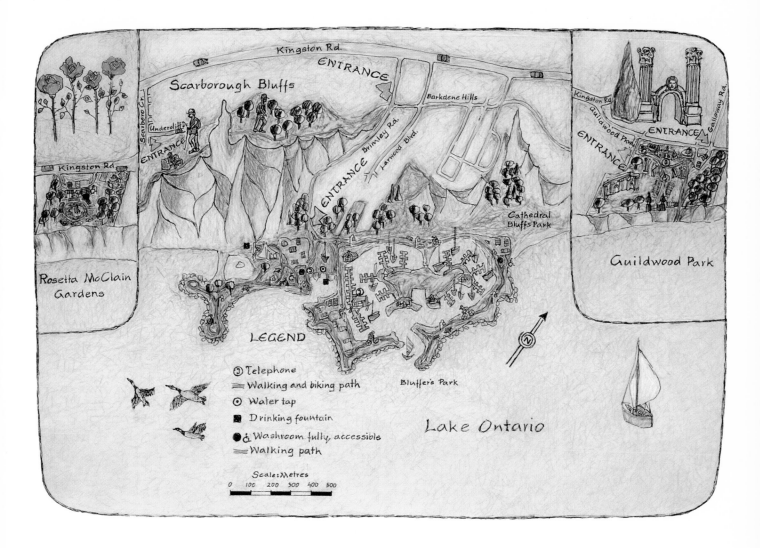

Kingston Rd.

ENTRANCE

Scarborough Bluffs

Barkdene Hills

Scarboro Cr.

Undercliff Dr.

ENTRANCE

Brimley Rd.

ENTRANCE

Larwood Blvd.

Kingston Rd.

Rosetta McClain
Gardens

Cathedral
Bluffs Park

Kingston Rd.

Guildwood Pkwy

ENTRANCE

Galloway Rd.

ENTRANCE

Guildwood Park

LEGEND

Bluffer's Park

N

Lake Ontario

| Telephone | Walking and biking path | Water tap | Drinking fountain | Washroom fully, accessible | Walking path |

Scale: Metres

0   100   200   300   400   500

Guildwood Park, October 1996

Scarborough Bluffs Park, November 1996

East Point Park, October 1996

A NOTE ON TECHNIQUE

All photographs for this book were taken with a 1950's 4x5 Crown Graphic view Camera. Like all old cameras it has its own soul. It has seen a lot. I love it for its light weight and simplicity.

Three different lenses were used for this project: 105mm, 135mm and 195mm. All of them are wonderful German Tessar designs manufactured in the 1910's. They are sharp but not too contrasty. With no anti-reflective coating, they seem to respect light much more than any modern lens.

To have full control of depth of field and exposure time I used a set of neutral density filters. Wanting to record the movement I rarely used exposure times shorter than one second; often as long as 30-40. For some of the photographs I used double or triple exposures.

Agfa APX 100 ASA film was exposed at either 25, 50 or 100 ASA depending on the contrast of a scene, and processed in Rodinal at 1:100 solution. For the purpose of this book, the prints were digitally scanned and then toned and tinted using Adobe Photoshop 4.0.

A.M.